# THE MANITOU PASSAGE STORY

An Indefinitive History of
the Settlement of Northeast Lake Michigan

Gene Warner

Copyright © 2007 – 2011 Gene L Warner
PO Box 604, Grand Haven, Michigan 49417-0604 USA
All rights reserved under International and Pan-American Copyright Conventions.

Published in the United States by

BoysMind Books
www.boysmindbooks.com

Book Description: Learn about the natural and human history of the Manitou Passage, from glacier to National Park! This small book offers a light, sometimes romantic, conspectus written in the conversational style of the popular broadcast series, "Alistair Cooke's America."

Publishers Cataloging in Publication Data

    Warner, Gene L.
    The Manitou Passage Story: An Indefinitive History of the Settlement of Northeast Lake Michigan – First Edition – rev January 2011

        3 5 7 9 0 8 6 4 2

    p. cm.
    Includes bibliographical references and index

    ISBN: 978-0-9797896-0-1

    1. Michigan – History. 2. Lake Michigan. 3. Manitou Islands. 4. Sleeping Bear Dunes National Lakeshore. I. Warner, Gene L. II. Title

F566.W37   2011           BISAC: HIS036090
977 – dc22                 LCCN: 2004106645

Author Website Address: www.boysmindbooks.com

*To Uncle "June"*
~
*Someone remembers.*

# Contents

Introduction .......................................................iii

The Wilderness ..................................................1
The Asians .........................................................3
New Faces in the Wilderness ..........................7
Spoils of War .....................................................9
New Owners ................................................... 11
The New Outpost ........................................... 13
Ships that Walked in the Water..................... 17
The Wooding Stations ................................... 21
The Crowded Sea ~ The Coming
    of Government Workers .......................... 29
The Settlers .................................................... 35
The Wilderness Returns ................................ 41
The Sleeping Bear Dunes
National Lakeshore ........................................ 49

Bibliography ................................................... 53
Index ............................................................... 55
About the Author........................................... 59

# Introduction

It wasn't really so long ago; it hardly seems right to refer to the story as "history." My great-great grandparents on my father's side were among the original settlers of South Manitou Island. The human history of the place began with their arrival, having lain as a pristine wilderness over the preceding ages. But that was only four generations ago, a scant 150-years. When I was a boy, their children were still living. We'd sometimes visit my great-grandparents on their island farm, giving hello hugs, and kissing them goodbye, never thinking we might be touching a part of history.

During the 1800's the nation expanded rapidly, thanks to the coming of waves of European immigrants. The Great Lakes route between Buffalo and Chicago carried more traffic than almost any other waterway in the country. About 150-miles out of Chicago, towards Lake Michigan's northeast end, nature provided a natural refuge and refueling area. It became strategically important to the commerce and travel going on with sailing vessels and steamboats.

It was called "The Manitou Passage."

# The Wilderness

As are most landscapes in the northern latitudes, the Great Lakes and their adjacent land features are the work of ancient glaciers. In prehistoric episodes of declining temperatures followed by global warming, ice sheets higher than many of today's mountains, alternately pushed their way south, then receded back from whence they came. Scraping, gouging and milling the earth under millions of tons of ice in their southward excursions, they roughed in the landscape's salient features. Then, gradually melting away, they left huge water-filled pits and piles of rubble as finishing touches. This was their legacy to creation.

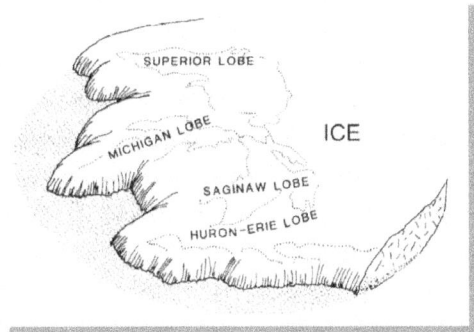

We foolish mortals, we arrogant "stewards of creation," are disposed to think that the earth as it is today is the way it ought to be; the product of creative efforts done on our behalf. When "our" lake rises or falls a few inches, playing havoc with some of our conveniences or contrivances, we become alarmed and call out our gurus to devise an explanation. The same self-importance usually leads us to the conclusion that, for some reason or another, such things are our fault.

Nevertheless, in its time, Lake Michigan has been much higher and much lower, once almost thirty feet higher and then again once almost 350-feet lower. Both epochs saw humans puttering around along the shores. In thinking we might belittle as a product of their ignorance and limited perspective, these early people might have felt the same way, fearing they had somehow displaced the "Great Spirit."

We live in a continuum of time. All of our generations have occupied only the briefest moment in time. We came to the Passage, we saw, we conquered. Nature abided. And now that our time here is through, she restores. In the larger view, we were clearly transients, johnny-come-latelies to a system which for thousands of years had existed quite successfully, thank you, without us. Now we leave, and we will not be missed.

The place we now call "the Manitou Passage" was, for thousands of years, a wilderness, unmolested by humans. A more advanced culture of early Americans is known to have lived here over 2,600 years ago, and may have actually been the area's first real settlers. They were able to subsist on what the wilderness provided; its plentiful game, fish and growing things being more than sufficient to their small numbers. The first "civilized" Caucasians came much later, but even when European white men did come, several factors worked in concert over the years to preserve the integrity of the wilderness – until the mid 1850's, only about 150-years ago.

# The Asians

What shall we call the aboriginal stone age people who wandered the shores of the ancient ancestral lakes textbooks now call Chicago, Algonquin, Chippewa, and Nipissing? Scholars call them Paleo-Indians but, of course, we understand that the idea of calling people on this continent "Indians" originated by mistake in 1492. Indians of today prefer to be called Native Americans, but their ancestors are thought to have come from Asia, migrating onto the North American continent over a land bridge  between today's Siberia and Alaska. So they too were immigrants; people who were not actually native to the area. It's all relative.

These Early Americans were, for millenniums, low impact users of creation. They hunted and gathered along the shores of "the big lake" for at least 11,000 years before the coming of European white men. Becoming somewhat more settled within tribal organizations, the Woodland Indians lived as small communities, following the game and harvest seasons, never growing large in numbers, never establishing any permanent, year-around settlements. Neither did they significantly alter or despoil the landscape, or decimate the populations of other living things. They were apparently content to live off the land, trading and occasionally warring between themselves. What would eventually become Michigan was the exclusive domain of the Ojibwa, Ottawa, Potawatomi and Huron until about 350-years ago.

As for the Manitou Passage, these people are thought to have seldom ventured off the mainland. There is some evidence of short-term island visitations over the centuries; simple encampments, nothing more. Since game was abundant on the mainland, and in pitifully short supply on the two virgin islands, the purpose of such visits can only be guessed. Perhaps it was simple curiosity. There was really very little else, as far as anyone knows, to entice anyone to bother mak-

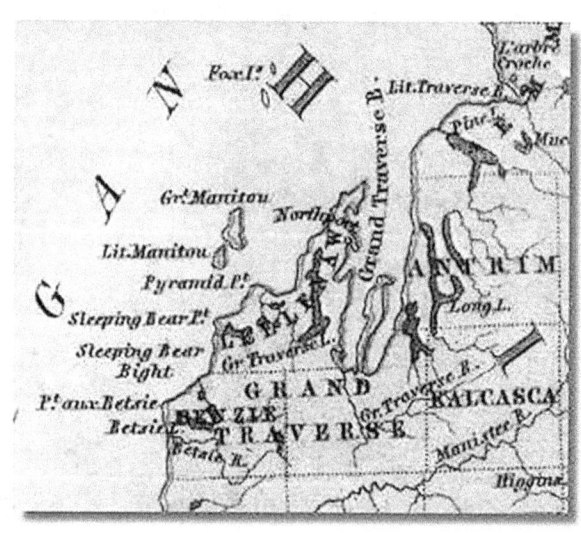

4   The Manitou Passage Story

ing the trip, as these early visitors presumably learned the hard way.

Legend has it that the Indians eventually came to view the islands as a sort of Bali Hai – enchanted places, the abode of their dead ancestors and the feared Great Spirit "Manitou". Thereafter they were apt to purposefully avoid these sacred places. That legend gave the islands their original names, *Great Manitou* and *Little Manitou*.

# New Faces in the Wilderness

The earliest Europeans to come were a breed who chose to coexist, rather than displace the existing residents. They were, for the most part, fur trappers, and mostly French. Many lived among, traded freely with, and even intermarried with the Indians. Like the Indians, they tended to be itinerants, rather than settlers. This was a time preceding an abundance of organic fibers, and inexpensive synthetic materials wouldn't be known for hundreds of years. Fur was important for the manufacture of essential clothing and hats, so the trade was jealously protected. French law forbade settlement in areas considered essential to the trade, which included the Lake Michigan area.

Roads that developed on the land were often laid over what had been ancient Indian trails. In a similar manner, travel on the Great Lakes initially followed routes traditionally used by the Indians in their seasonal migrations and trading junkets. Since prevailing westerly winds made for rough and sometimes dangerous waters on the east side of Lake Michigan, the Indians had traditionally kept to the other side, skirting the more placid shorelines of what we now call Michigan's Upper Peninsula, Wisconsin and Illinois. For the same reason, and also because of the geographical location of their vast fur trapping/trading enterprises in the Mississippi River basin, from what is now Minnesota and the Dakotas to New Orleans, the French followed suit. The Michigan shoreline was quite devoid of any sign of civilization, and was therefore visited only very occasionally and only by the most adventurous or foolhardy white men.

Some Indian tribes were less receptive to the white man's intrusion. In time, the maturing of the fur trade brought higher orders of civilization into the area around Lakes Erie and Ontario, including a horde of Jesuit priests burning with missionary zeal and bent on saving the souls of the region's savages. Most of the Indian nations accepted their gifts and ministrations, perhaps with some ambivalence. The Iroquois, who had traditionally been at odds with the white man's encroachment, did not. They found this disrespect of their beliefs, customs and culture, and the Jesuits' efforts to replace them, patently offensive. The result was what the French called the Iroquois League.

In the late 1650's a group of five Iroquois tribes, with the assistance of Dutch fur merchants, joined forces to oust the French from their tribal lands and end their control of the fur trade. Tribes friendly to the French became the enemy of the Iroquois, leading to raids on their villages, as well as French settlements. As the Iroquois war parties pursued more friendly tribes into Michigan's Lower Peninsula, the place quickly became known as a no man's land. The Iroquois threat was finally and viciously disposed of in the fall of 1665. But Michigan's reputation as a place of high-risk travel persisted for many years, further discouraging anyone from moving into the area permanently.

# Spoils of War

In the mid-eighteenth century, the British, French and other European empires had a go at each other in a long, vicious encounter, prompted mostly by conflicting colonial claims. The Seven Years War prompted the French on this side of the sea to seize the moment to once and for all confine the English colonies to the eastern seaboard, and end their incursions into what the French considered as their territory. The sporadic encounters on this side of the sea, between British colonial troops (and ultimately British regulars) and the French with their Indian allies, came to be called "the French and Indian War" in American history books.

The greater war between the European powers ended with a treaty in 1763 that altered their territorial claims on the other side of the Atlantic and elsewhere, with the French loosing much of their territory on the North American continent.

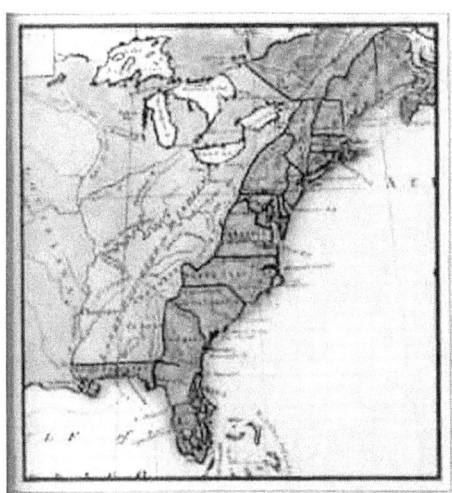

Among other changes, the Great Lakes region became British territory. Because of the fur trade, this was seen as a valuable concession.

Unlike the French, the British managed their fur trade in a structured and hierarchical way. The trapping function was provided mainly by Indians, whose pelts were purchased at prices set by the buyers, who then resold them for ten times as much, reaping handsome profits.

Much to the consternation of the British fur merchants, the unruly American colonists had little respect for their monopolistic and exploitative system, trapping when and where they pleased, and entering into more competitive deals with the Indians. A result was that the British officially declared all of their holdings west of the Allegheny Mountains as "Lands Reserved for the Indians," as shown on an official map (above) distributed by the British in 1763. This acted as a continuation of the French policy forbidding emigration and settlement.

# NEW OWNERS

This situation finally ended with the defeat of the British at the end of the American Revolution in 1776. The emerging American government had different priorities than the European monarchs and businessmen. Power was centered in the thirteen original colonies along the eastern seaboard, with little representation for the hinterlands west of the Allegheny ridges. Southern interests were more apt to concern themselves with maximizing cotton exports. Northern interests were more often expansionist, with an eye to establishing a broad commerce in other commodities.

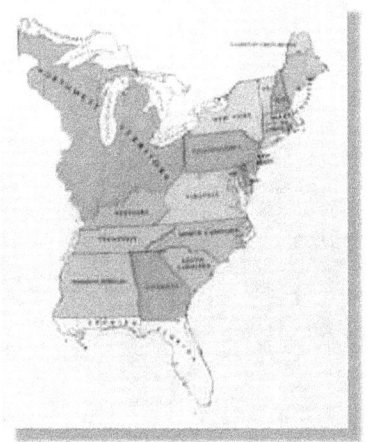

The formerly lucrative fur trade had entered its period of decline, diminishing in importance as the driving force of human activity in the Great Lakes region. Many of the original colonies had laid claim to portions of the newly acquired lands on the other side of the coastal mountain ranges, and disputes arose which were making it all but impossible to finalize the creation of a union. In 1781 a compromise was finally reached wherein everyone relinquished their claims, permitting the newly designated *Northwest Territory* to become the corporate property of the union. Proceeds from the sale of lands in this territory were to be used to foster immigration, and to fund an army sufficient to the security interests of the region, and the new nation.

The British however, remained nominally in control of the area for another twenty years, their presence finally and permanently ending following the War of 1812. Thus also ended the long period of official protectionism and superstition that had kept Michigan a dark, foreboding wilderness.

In former centuries, events and circumstances had always conspired to keep settlers out of the area. Within the next several decades, just the opposite was destined to occur. More change would be seen here in the next hundred-years than had occurred in the 10,000 years preceding it.

History was in the making.

# The New Outpost

In the early 1800's the area to the south and west of Michigan's lower peninsula saw much increased settlement by immigrant farmers. The city of Chicago began to develop as a major distribution center for commodities produced in this area. During these times, travel by land was still difficult and uncomfortable. Wherever possible, natural waterways were exploited as the nation's highways; and wherever not possible, man began to make it possible by constructing canals which connected rivers and lakes, and short-cut river meanders. This canal-building craze of the early 1800's produced, among many others, the Erie Canal, which officially opened in 1825.

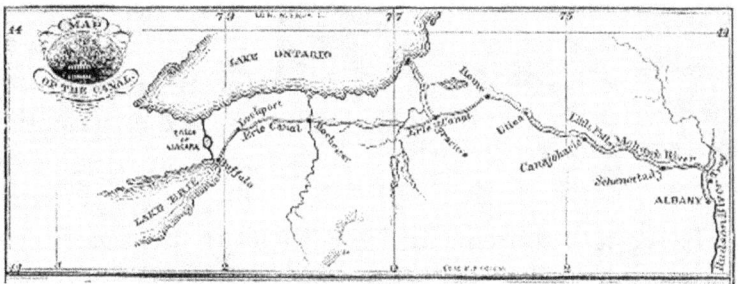

The brainstorm of New York's Governor Dewitt Clinton, and sometimes dubbed "Clinton's Folly" by its detractors, this 400-mile canal linked Albany on the upper Hudson River, to Buffalo at the eastern end of Lake Erie. This made it possible to travel by water from New York City to Chicago. In 1816 Clinton predicted –

> *"As an organ of communication between the Hudson, the Mississippi, the St. Lawrence, the Great Lakes of the north and west and their tributary rivers, it will create the greatest inland trade ever witnessed."*

This probably came very close to being perfectly prophetic. The canal was an immediate success, teeming with horse-drawn freight barges and passenger boats called "packets." It was expanded several times within a very few years, to accommodate the ever-increasing number and size of canal boats. The cost of shipping commodities by boat fell to about a tenth of what it cost to ship overland. This made it feasible to ship bulk general cargo from Chicago to points east, and even to export markets through the port of New York, which quickly became the major port city on the east coast.

Traffic on the Great Lakes increased exponentially after the opening of this waterway. Skirting the western shoreline of Lake Michigan was clearly not the most direct route for ships traveling between Chicago and Buffalo. Taking a shortcut through the island chain in the northeast part of the lake offered the advantage of shortening the journey by some seventy miles. Although this was still a wilderness area on the land, as more and more ship captains decided to risk the Manitou Passage, this route became fairly civilized in the sea-lanes by virtue of all the other traffic in the area. In a very short time, because of the time and cost savings, this became the route of choice for through ships.

In the early days, South Manitou Island was an important asset to those plying this route because of the bay on its southeast side. This large, deep-water bay offered ships of all sizes safe harbor from the ravages of the lake when stormy weather blew in, typically from the northwest. This was doubly important because of the fact that the waters in this particular area are also quite treacherous, featuring a number of sandy shoals and rocky shores.

For sailing ships, the very force that ordinarily powered the vessel could quickly render it non-maneuverable and drive it into dangerous waters. Safe harbors were therefore an essential consideration for any route being contemplated, and South Manitou was the best bet in  this particular area. During these times, it was not uncommon for the bay to quickly fill up with sailing ships, which put in to ride out foul weather at anchor in its calm waters. When the winds were easterly, the bay sometimes offered little protection, but an alternative was only three or four miles away. The deep waters and the broad, high bluffs on the west side of North Manitou provided ample protection from such blows.

# Ships That Walked in the Water

History books most often cite the Canadian *Frontenac* as the first steamship on the Great Lakes, and the American *Walk-In-The-Water* as the first American steamship to sail these inland seas. Apparently neither claim is actually valid. The Frontenac had a rather checkered and colorful history, which included running aground on her maiden voyage, being acquired by the Hamiltons (Alexander Hamilton and his brother) in her old age, and ultimately meeting her end in a mysterious blaze. The Walk-In-The-Water may have won her place in history simply by a fortuitous choice of names, supposedly taken from the expression Indians used at the time to describe such boats, which, in itself, suggests she probably wasn't the first they'd seen.

The Frontenac appeared in 1816, and a year later was running a regular passenger and freight route the length of Lake Ontario between Prescott and Burlington. The Walk-in-the-Water was launched at Black Rock, near Buffalo, in 1818, and is credited as being the first steamboat to sail Lake Erie and the upper Great Lakes. She ran between Buffalo and Detroit for three seasons, but because she had been so expensive to build, she failed to make a profit. In an attempt to extend her earnings, her owners operated her late into the year of 1821, setting sail for Cleveland and Detroit on the last day of October. By evening, Lake Erie was in the grip of a fierce gale. Her captain dropped anchor and prepared for a rough night, but several anchor lines snapped, and the boat was savagely tossed ashore. Passengers and crew were saved, and her engine and fittings were salvaged for use in two later steamboats.

These first generation steamships might have more accurately been referred to as steam-assisted ships. Their simple one-cylinder engines were noisy, dirty and grossly inefficient. The fuel load itself constituted a significant cargo, and turning the huge sidewheels spent much of the power these small engines were able to develop. Their steam engine was intended primarily as a means of addressing the age-old problem of calm. Sails work very nicely when the winds are brisk and favorable, which they typically are on the Great Lakes during daylight hours in the summer months. But with sunset, sails would go slack, the water calmed and the serenity of "red sails in the sunset" often prevailed. Ships were apt to simply sit dead in the water for ten hours or so, from dusk 'til dawn. This was accepted as a simple fact of the mariner's life; it had been this way since sails replaced oars. But it had now suddenly become possible to defeat the calm, and remain underway, perhaps making six to nine knots at the most. But sixty to ninety miles a night added up, and these engines could significantly shorten travel times for long voyages. It's easy to see why, in a very short span of years, about a third of the vessels on the Great Lakes were ships of this type.

*Walk in the Water* — 1818

In 1841, an odd-looking boat named the *Vandalia* appeared on the Great Lakes. She was built like a small sloop with a clipper ship bow, and but for the small stack near her stern, she gave every impression of being a conventional sailing ship. There were no paddle wheels on her sides, yet she moved handily through the water even with no sails set.

The Vandalia was the first Great Lakes implementation of the screw propeller, the invention of a Swede named John Ericsson. This design produced boats that were quieter and much more fuel-efficient, and set the standard for future ship design. Around 1860, there were about 1,450 registered commercial vessels working the Great Lakes. Some 1,100 of these were still sailing vessels – schooners, ketches, sloops and barkentines – with the remaining 350 being steamers and propellers. At this point, propeller driven boats outnumbered the far less efficient side-wheelers by almost two to one.

# The Wooding Stations

These ships were fueled by wood and had a voracious appetite for it. This gave rise to a new industry on the Great Lakes; cutting stovewood and refueling steamships. Logging-refueling stations appeared wherever there was a good supply of hardwood near a good natural harbor. One such place was South Manitou Island. Much of the traffic in the Manitou Passage involved shipping between Chicago and Buffalo. The island, which had been known as a primary port of refuge for many years, and the only natural port in the 300-miles between the Straits of Mackinaw and Chicago, was ideally located as the first wooding stop for Buffalo-bound ships, and the last one for the Chicago-bound traffic.

In the early days of the steamboat era, ships entered South Manitou's deepwater bay and their crews would go ashore to set about the work of chopping and loading stovewood for their boilers. In 1835 Captain Hubbard Burton and his brother William landed on the island and established a wooding station. Although their initial occupancy was probably seasonal, William Burton and his family are generally accorded the distinction as the island's first permanent residents and entrepreneurs, and were probably the first in the region known as the Manitou Passage. Their venture prospered, and within a few years South Manitou had virtually monopolized the refueling business. A passenger on one of the many vessels stopping here "to wood" wrote about the island's loggers, describing them as scruffy ruffians who lived in crude huts and spent most of their off-time drinking and gambling away their earnings. That account was picturesque, but evidently not accurate.

Within a dozen years, the Burtons had established civilization on the island at a point near the middle of its bay which became known as Burton's Wharf. A state survey party working on the island in 1847 recorded a dock, a general store, a blacksmith shop and a three-mile wooden railway (used to move logs from the forest to the dock area.) 

This small village on the shores of Crescent Bay was the first pioneer settlement in the area, which was still a wilderness. It was inhabited mostly by the Burtons' loggers, and other individuals who worked in supporting roles or other enterprises connected with the boat traffic. It also became a trading post, with Indians making the crossing in their canoes from *Mishimigobing* on the mainland (Leland) to trade in Burtons' store. William Burton was never able to purchase or otherwise legally acquire any property on the island until after it was finally surveyed by the government in 1847, so for some 14-years the Burtons were preempting, as it were, publicly owned land. Back in that day, in contrast with today's ways of thinking, clear-cutting forests was considered as "improving the land." Moreover, maritime traffic being considered essential to the growth of the nation, the strategically located Burton operation was seen as an important public service. Burton and his sons continued as the island's major businessmen for another 40-years. By the 1880's most steamships had converted from wood to coal, and the island's era as a refueling stop had come to its end.

The Burtons sold off their holdings prior to the turn of the century, the elders having passed on, and the children having scattered between Cleveland, Detroit, Chicago, California and the Pacific northwest.

During the Burtons' time, South Manitou became a regularly scheduled stop for ships whose business took them through the Passage. These boats became familiar sights as they entered the bay, their operators and crewmen, familiar faces. An at-large community of mariners had developed on Lake Michigan, and South Manitou became one of its centers.

The Burton operation on South Manitou had been the first of several similar enterprises that sprang up in the area. Nicholas Pickard came to North Manitou Island when he was about twenty-seven, a wood agent for his Uncle who operated steamboats out of Buffalo. He established a similar operation on the north island probably about 1845, and by 1847 he had some forty woodcutters working for him. In 1849 he built his first dock near the southern tip on the east side of the island. Like Burton, he was "improving" public domain land, a practice considered laudable in these times. By 1860, at age forty-three, he had become wealthy enough to have acquired over 1,200 acres on the island, holding logging rights on much of the rest.

At some point Pickard apparently felt that the physical characteristics of the north island gave him a special advantage over the Burton operation on the south island, and he built a second dock on the island's west side, a few miles north of South Manitou's northern-most shores. Steamships wishing to avoid the passage by sailing around the north and west sides of the island then became his customers, as did those arriving during times when easterly winds made sailing into South Manitou's bay chancy. This proved to be a marginal venture. Shortly before 1860 he sold the dock to a mainlander, who closed it down thirteen years later. The little settlement that had developed here ultimately became the area's first ghost town. The north island probably saw its most prosperous decade during the 1860's. In the decade that followed, business declined, there being only one wood merchant left on the island by 1880. Pickard lived to be about sixty years old, dying about 1877.

In 1862 Thomas Kelderhouse, already a successful businessman and ship owner, noticing the area's unique geographical advantage and business potential on his voyages through the passage, built a dock on the mainland just south of Pyramid Point. One of the first steamships to dock at this place was the S. S. Oneida, and the place then became known as Port Oneida. Over the next twenty-five to thirty years, Kelderhouse continued to acquire land, and the town grew to include a sawmill, a blacksmith shop, a boarding house, general store and post office, two barns and the Kelderhouse home itself. Kelderhouse died in 1884, and the business passed to his children. By the 1890's the Kelderhouses had chopped and shipped most of the wood that was available in the area, and most of the steamships on the Great Lakes were now burning coal. The dock and sawmill went on the block and were sold off in the early 1890's. By 1908, all the buildings in what had been the town of Port Oneida were abandoned, except for the Kelderhouse home, which was occupied by one of the sons. So the empire built by Thomas Kelderhouse lasted only about thirty years.

October 8, 1871 is loosely known as "The Day Michigan Burned." Some forty towns burned to the ground on that day. Glen Haven was one of them. The town, some say was originally called "Sleeping Bearville," had been established on Sleeping Bear Bay by Charles McCarthy in the 1850's. An inn was built in 1863, and a 100-yard long dock was constructed in two years later. With these fine facilities,

Glen Haven became one of the busiest steamship stops on the Great Lakes. In 1870, the Northern Transportation Company (NTC) bought Glen Haven and the cordwood operation, to service their fleet of 24 steamships.

A year later, on that "Black Sunday" which also spawned the infamous Great Chicago Fire, fires raged all along the shores of Lakes Michigan and Huron, from Illinois, through Wisconsin and into the Upper Peninsula, then around the top of the mitten and into the thumb area. As the smoke from these conflagrations drifted out into the lakes and settled over the cooler waters, navigation became difficult at best, and impossible in some areas, resulting in a rash of groundings, collisions and shipwrecks. Some called the fires God's wrath, fearing the end times had arrived. Others blamed them on freak lightning storms, and still others on a shower of meteors. The facts were probably less dramatic.

In 1871 the wooding business along the lakeshores was at its peak. Simultaneously, the railroad business was rapidly developing; some just small lines of track belonging to the loggers, while others operated larger inter-city systems carrying paying passengers and freight. Both businesses tended to be paternalistic, with the livelihoods of those living in their service areas tied closely to their operations. Few were willing to challenge or criticize their operations or methods if, in fact, they ever gave it any thought. For their part, the loggers ran chop and slash operations, leaving piles and debris and slashings in their logging areas, and sawdust everywhere else, from the mills to the docks. Roads were frequently paved with the plentiful sawdust, its resins helping to stabilize their sandy substrate. Others were covered with wood scraps to tighten them up. Areas in towns around the mills and at the docks were littered with stockpiles of chord wood and sometimes shingles and finished lumber. NTC, with their major dock in Glen Haven, had become one of the largest wooding operations in the area, so this scene was no doubt the Glen Haven of 1871.

Meanwhile, like the steamboats, the railroads of this period also burned wood in their locomotives, showering sparks and embers in their wake as they sped along their tracks. The interesting shapes of the large smoke stacks seen on early locomotives reflects the serious work that was being done on developing spark arrestors for these machines. Nevertheless, locomotives were notorious for starting brush and forest fires, and more than half of such fires were attributed to railroad operations. Like many others, NTC

owned its own tracks, and ran its own locomotives to carry logs from the woods to the mills and the dock.

The late summer of 1871 had been unusually hot and dry. Scant rainfall during the months of August and September had turned these areas into tinderboxes, waiting for the slightest hint of flame to set them off. During the afternoon that fateful day, the winds turned around to the southwest, and gathered in intensity to near hurricane force. Once kindled, the blazes almost instantly grew far beyond the rudimentary fire fighting abilities of the company and local residents.

Firestorms moved rapidly through the forests and towns. These tornadoes of fire, easily jumped clearings and streams, spewing large pieces of burning material into the air, some of which was later found as far as twenty or thirty miles from its original location. Air temperatures increased beyond the kindling temperature of dried-out boards, and buildings with no sign of fire immediately nearby could suddenly explode into flame and burn to the ground. Roads which had been improved with sawdust, bark or wood also burst into flame, blocking escape routes. There was little anyone could do but hurriedly gather up prized belongings and important papers and run to the beach, seeking safety at the water's edge and helplessly watching their town burn down.

In a bitter enigma of the sort which sometimes seems all too common in life, torrential rains came the very next day.

There had, of course, been fires in the area before, and others would follow. But none ever had, nor ever would, match the epic proportions of those that began on Sunday, October 8, 1871. The loss of lives was numbered in the thousands, the loss of buildings in the tens of thousands and the loss of fortunes in the hundreds of millions; not to mention the personal tragedies of those who lost loved ones, and everything they had accumulated during their lifetime.

Forest and brush fires were, and still are, a more or less natural phenomenon. But the sad statistics resulting from the fires of 1871 can be attributed largely to the production and consumption of wood, either as a cheap, readily available fuel, or as a plentiful and inexpensive building material. From this point of view, the fires of Black Sunday might be seen as another contribution the loggers made to the area's history.

# THE CROWDED SEA ~ THE COMING OF GOVERNMENT WORKERS

By the mid-1800's, Lake Michigan was teeming with traffic. Chicago had already developed into an important commodity-trading center, and boasted the largest corn market in the country. During the three peak months of the 1869 shipping season, the port of Chicago logged over 12,000 departures and arrivals. Much of this traffic was headed for, or arriving from, the eastern Great Lakes, via the Manitou Passage. Other settlements also began to spring up all along the lakeshore, on both sides, wherever an improvable natural harbor offered a convenient on-ramp to this busy aquatic expressway.

The growth and economic importance of this shipping traffic prompted the government to take an interest in facilitating navigation and promoting safety on the Lakes. As a first step, a system of beacons was developed, with a lighthouse appearing at just about every port or prominence along the lakeshores. Eventually, Michigan would be equipped with a total of 116 lighthouses. The first lighthouse on Lake Michigan was built at Chicago and became operational in the fall of 1834.

The first light provided for the Manitou Passage went into operation on South Manitou Island in the autumn six years later. William N. Burton, the eldest son of the Burton family, was appointed by the government as its first Keeper, at a salary of $350 per year. He held the post for about two and a half years, being replaced by a new appointee in spring of 1843. Thus began a succession of Keepers which numbered seventeen during the lighthouse's 95-years of service. Counting first and second assistants, the facility actually employed some forty-nine men in its time, some of them islanders and some that came to the island after being assigned to the post of "Keeper" by the *U.S. Lighthouse Establishment* in Washington D.C. Most of these brought families to the island. So with the coming of the Lighthouse Establishment came a new class of settlers – government workers.

Ships navigating the Manitou Passage doubtless knew all too well that they were sailing dangerous waters. In what appears to be open water, depths vary widely and erratically from as little as 24-feet on sandy and rocky shoals to over 200-feet in the channel. During stormy weather, huge swells effectively reduce the depths on the shoals such that any boat blundering or being helplessly blown out of the deep channel was likely to meet its end here. And many did. There are over two-hundred and fifty shipwrecks lying on the bottom in this area.

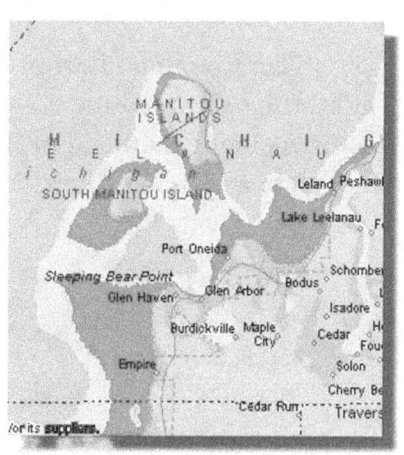

But if the passage presented dangers, it also provided fuel and shelter. Sleeping Bear Bay, South Manitou's "Crescent Bay," and the southwest side of North Manitou could shelter ships from any blow, the best anchorage depending upon where the storm was coming from. The worst weather was apt to come from a westerly direction, making South Manitou's natural deep-water harbor the usual choice. It therefore made more sense to sail the passage, rather than to navigate around the north side of the islands.

Along with increasing shipping came an increasing number of disasters, with shipwrecks and loss of life on the Great Lakes matching those on the Atlantic. A series of maritime disasters in the New York coastal area brought the situation to crisis proportions in 1848, and the government responded by providing surfboats and lifesaving equipment in the hands of volunteers at key points along the coast. Six years later, similar equipment was provided around the Great Lakes.

The volunteer idea didn't prove to be very effective, and Congress then moved to provide funding for regularly paid, if still untrained and undisciplined, crews. Finally, in 1878 the government established the *United States Life Saving Service* as a branch of the Treasury Department. The act also addressed the issues of training and discipline, resulting in a professional service with the assigned mission of saving lives and property in cases of shipwreck.

The golden era of shipping on the Great Lakes spanned the years from the end of the Civil War in the 1860's into the 1890's. In 1869 a four-day storm ended the lives of some ninety-seven ships. An October gale in 1880 destroyed ninety boats, claiming 188 lives in the process. In the twenty years between 1878 and 1898, some six thousand ships fell victim to storms on the Great Lakes. Passage of the bill creating the USLSS came late, and its implementation was not immediate. Years passed while studies were made, the best locations for facilities often being very difficult for people to agree on.

One such dispute arose between those wanting a station on Sleeping Bear and others who thought it best located on South Manitou Island. In the end, the decision was finally made to build stations at both locations. Meanwhile, the first Life Saving Station in the passage had already been built on North Manitou in 1877, on land leased to the government by Nicholas Pickard. A relatively ineffective lighthouse was built on the southern end of North Manitou in 1898, marking its main shoal, which ran due south from that point. In 1910, the lightship *Manitou* was anchored at the end of the shoal, rendering the North Manitou light of little further value.

The Sleeping Bear and South Manitou Lifesaving Stations were finally opened just after the turn of the century. But it was too little; too late. By this time the days of the sailing ships and early steamboats were coming to an end, being replaced by a smaller number of much larger, faster and safer "propellers." In 1915 the Life Saving Service was combined with the Revenue Cutter Service to form the United States Coast Guard. Several years later, the U.S. Lighthouse Service was also merged into the Coast Guard.

As with the Lighthouses, the Life Saving Stations on Sleeping Bear, South Manitou and North Manitou, during their active years, provided employment for many of the area's residents. There was work to be done provisioning these facilities, and local young men often won appointments as Assistant Keepers or Surfmen. New people were also transferred here from other locations. The government, through the establishment of these services and these facilities, therefore played an important, if indirect, role in the settlement of these places. Members of lighthouse keepers' or servicemen's families often developed permanent connections here, deciding to stay even after their term of service had ended. In other cases, departing  government workers took with them memories and stories of these places, and sometimes brides, as they moved to other locations around the Great Lakes, putting them on the map within the close community of the U.S. Coast Guard.

Ironically, although the role played by these quasi-military outfits is often relegated to side-bar status in historical writings about the area, it is these very facilities and their stories – the lighthouses and Coast Guard installations – that people seem most interested in preserving and interpreting. They have therefore become featured attractions in what is now the Sleeping Bear Dunes National Lakeshore.

# The Settlers

The story of the settlers who moved into the land area surrounding the Manitou Passage is mostly one of German immigrants. Germany, having previously seen ages of capable leadership which had enabled a placid life for her peoples and epic advances in the arts and sciences, entered into what was destined to be a long period of turmoil and travail following Martin Luther's reformation movement. The country was first devastated by the *Thirty Years War* (1618 ~ 1648), with the loss of over three-quarters of its 17-million people, either killed, else dying of starvation or disease. Some fifty years later, Louis XIV ordered the French to invade and lay waste to as much of the country as possible.  German Princes, either bent on appeasement or simply wishing to emulate the opulence of the French court, began to subjugate their people socially and economically, often suspending religious choice.

In 1756, during the *Seven Years War* several of her neighboring nations attempted to divide the kingdom of Frederick the Great and finally, in 1798, Napoleon subjugated and plundered the country, dismantling the empire and distributing the individual German states to cronies. He was eventually defeated by an alliance of common Germans and Austrians at Leipzig, and many of the Germans expected this would finally open the way to social reform and democracy. But their hopes were dashed as the resurgent leadership chose to return to the old status quo. This led to a smoldering popular unrest, which finally reached its climax and flared up in open conflict in the 1840's. This was more of a rebellion than a revolution and, being poorly organized and orchestrated, was lost in 1848.

Each of these calamities sent waves of German immigrants to America's shores. Over two centuries, between about 1609 and 1790, over 100,000 Germans came into the country. The 1850's produced massive waves of German immigration, with 215,000 arriving in 1854 alone. By 1860, there were an estimated 1.3-million German-born immigrants in America. The peak German immigration occurred

in the 1880's, when 1.5-million Germans left for the United States, 1/4-million in 1882 alone.

In the last half of the nineteenth century, European immigration became a popular and profitable business. Recruiters roamed the countryside distributing literature extolling the virtues of America. Some represented legitimate interests, such as those dispatched by the State of Michigan to seek new high-quality settlers. Some others represented religious groups bent on bringing wretched European Protestants to this land of religious tolerance. But many were marketing people, representing ship owners who busied themselves building more and larger vessels to take advantage of the burgeoning demand. Immigrants came from most all of the countries in northern and western Europe – Finns, Norwegians, Swedes, Dutch, even some English and French. But the overwhelming majority were from the German provinces. In some instances, almost the whole population of small German villages disappeared. Local German governments and police officials also occasionally took advantage of the situation, mixing gangs of convicted criminals and vagrants in with the hoards of legitimate immigrant families, shipping them off to America to get rid of them once and for all.

Having arrived in America, many of these immigrants headed inland, seeking the opportunities on the frontier they'd been told about. Of necessity, they usually sought immediate employment, taking jobs wherever they could find them. Those who happened to wind up in Buffalo, then the gateway to the west, were apt to find work on ships making the run between there and Chicago, and would thereby come to know the Manitou Passage. Much is sometimes made of the immigrant families who decided to settle here, with reasons for their choice ranging from the aesthetic to the geographical similarities with their homeland. It seems more likely that for most it was a matter of happenstance. The logging operations were probably the main draw. If these operations were remote and rustic, they also offered employment at a decent wage to those having no trade – a chance to get ahead.

Some of the immigrants came here skilled in a trade; a blacksmith, a cooper, a carpenter. But the sparse population of the area made it a poor place to market such skills. Those who longed to be independent and self-sufficient had little else to turn to but farming. Because land was essentially free, some made that choice sooner, rather than later. As the wood merchants on the islands and the mainland closed down, one after another, there was little else to turn to other than farming. It was either that, or move on. If few came with that ambition originally in mind, it would only stand to reason, since the land here was typically poor. Those skilled in the art and looking for a place to settle for that purpose were more likely to head for the much more fertile lands of Ohio, Indiana, Illinois, Wisconsin, and Iowa, or even the southern and eastern sections of the Michigan mainland. And, of course, many did just that. Farming at the water's edge in the Manitou Passage area was mostly subsistence agriculture. In some cases farmers were able to produce small marketable surpluses. While ships were still stopping here to wood, moving these to market was relatively simple and inexpensive. But when the ships stopped coming, special arrangements had to be made to ship locally grown commodities and produce to big-city markets, and it usually wasn't worthwhile to do so.

South Manitou is probably the only place in the area between Sleeping Bear Point and Pyramid Point where there was any noteworthy agricultural achievement. This resulted because of its singular isolation, and as a result of experimentation being conducted by the state's first agricultural  college, which is today's Michigan State University. In short, researchers at the college were working with a Siberian strain of rye, which promised to double yields if only it could be protected from cross-pollination with other strains. South Manitou's isolation from the mainland made it the perfect place to conduct such experiments, and the island's few farmers were sold on the proposition of growing *Rosen Rye* exclusively. The experiment was a resounding success, and this strain of rye quickly caught on as a favored cash crop of seed grain. In a similar experiment, farmers on South Manitou were instrumental in the development of a very successful bean hybrid called the *Michelite Bean*.

Were it not for this niche business, farming on South Manitou would have no doubt suffered the same demise, in the same time frame, as that on the north island and the mainland. As it were, South Manitou's farmers proved to be the most steadfast. Farming on North Manitou was less so, going through periods of development and decline with different waves of immigrants; first the Germans, then the Scandinavians.

Farming on the mainland developed in the area known as Port Oneida after the demise of the logging industry there. But the land was mostly so poor that it was barely able to produce at subsistence levels, and farmers typically worked other jobs to earn the money that bought necessities they were not able to produce for themselves. Eventually, the improved production of successful farming operations elsewhere in the nation and improvements in transportation ren-  dered even subsistence farming more trouble than it was worth, and farming in the area gradually died as younger family members decided not to follow in their parents' footsteps. By 1950, farming in the area was, for all practical purposes, a thing of the past.

All in all, Port Oneida's farming community existed for only about fifty years, involving just two generations. It was typically the third generation of the early settlers' families who died on, and with, these farms. Fourth generation descendants moved away to urban areas and into careers which seemed to promise a better life. The old home places where they grew up gradually became little more than charming vistas on the pastoral landscape.

# The Wilderness Returns

Few accounts of the demise of this area give any credit to World War II. Yet this historic event may well have sealed its fate.

People here were already struggling to make ends meet as the dark clouds began to loom on the eastern horizon in the mid-1930's. The business of chopping stove wood for steamship boilers had long since totally died. Some of the logging operations converted to producing finished lumber, but the only appreciable stands of timber were on North Manitou Island, and they were quickly consumed. Logging had  been the only industry of any significance the area had ever seen, and its only reason for being here was because this was where the wood was. Industry was otherwise apt to locate closer to its sources of raw materials and its market, either physically or in terms of transportation services, and that meant mostly in or near growing cities far to the south.

Nobody gave any thought at all to the tourist trade. Traveling long distances in the family automobile for leisure was a recreation the future would bring. Most families didn't own an automobile, and those who did were most likely to be driving a *Model A* Ford, or even an older *Model T*. Highways were narrow and poorly graded, even roads that were paved, which were few and far between. Besides that, most of the country was still living outside of cities, or in very small towns. This majority of Americans had yet to experience the crowding and pressures of the urban lifestyle that drives today's tourists to seek beauty and quiet in far-away places.

For those who lived here, there was very little left except farming. As hopeless as that alternative was, the lack of money narrowed their choices. Most owned the land they lived on, but it wasn't much of an asset. Stripped of its trees and marginal at best for farming, who'd want to buy it? But, poor as it might be, their land assured their survival if worse came to worse. As long as they were still able to work it, starvation or a one-way trip to the county poor farm was unlikely.

Perhaps the most noteworthy aspect of World War II was the lasting impact it had on our society. World War II was the ultimate perfecteor of the Industrial Revolution. As is the usual case with war, might made right, but in this case it was economic might that carried the day. America was rich in natural resources, sheltered by distance from the rav-

ages of combat, and in possession of a fine labor force – much of it having previously immigrated from what was now to be enemy territory. Because of these advantages, we simply outlasted the adversaries.

Some eight million of America's young men, and 90,000 young women entered the service during this time. Those who remained behind found that employment suddenly came easy, with most jobs paying far more for work much easier than farming.

The country's industry cranked up as it never had before, and many fortunes were made supporting wartime production. At the end of the war, almost seven million of these service people found themselves honorably discharged from the military and looking for civilian work. The nation's factories also found themselves looking for work, and unemployment soared. The adjustment finally came as industry began to convert war-related technology and production methods to consumer products; things no subsistence farmer would ever be able to afford. Sons and daughters who had been away from the Manitou Passage during the war years now often found themselves reluctant to return, for the old home place up north had developed an image: "Sure, it's nice, but there's just no way to make a living up there."

By 1950, anyone visiting one of the area's farmsteads would be likely to find only the old folks still on the place. The conversation might eventually turn to their children, and they'd glow as they'd boast of their success in far-away places. Like the listener, their children had become visitors.

Little by little, the farms and the businesses which depended upon them, shut down. Unkempt outbuildings began to weather and roofs began to sag. Native overgrowth began to reclaim little two-track farm roads, pastures and production fields. The sounds of pastured livestock disappeared, and tractors rusted in barnyards. The days of "Farming on the Water's Edge" had come to an end, and Mother Nature was taking back much of what the early immigrants had worked so hard to wrest from her.

Changing demographics slowly began to bring changes to this situation. Working families in cities looked for weekend trips offering what the cities sorely lacked – beauty, space, peace and quiet. Roads were much improved and personal vehicles were comfortable, reliable and affordable. Sunday drives and weekend trips of a few hundred miles became a favorite American pastime.

Because of its lush natural beauty and the awesome Sleeping Bear sand dunes, Leelanau County, "Michigan's Little Finger," became an increasingly popular destination for such trips. Along with these visitors came the small scale entrepreneurs, selecting choice locations for gas stations, pop stands, small motels, miniature golf courses, dune rides, souvenir shops, dairy treats, and other enterprises aiming to exploit a growing tourist trade. Some of these small businesses were owned and operated by local residents, who welcomed the opportunities that tourism was bringing into the area. Others, especially those involving larger investments, were owned by outsiders whose only interest in the area was commercial. By the late 1950's it was plain that this unregulated development was rapidly displacing the area's chief assets; its pristine beauty and peaceful vistas.

In 1961, U.S. Senator Philip A Hart of Michigan introduced legislation to add the Sleeping Bear Dunes area to America's National Park system. The bill ultimately called for the eminent domain acquisition of some 77,000 acres, and property belonging to some 1,600 people, much of which represented homesteads that had been in families

 through several generations. Many who lived in the area feared that the federal government would confiscate their homes at prices reflecting the failed farming economy, rather than recognizing its increasing value as a result of the expanding tourism. On the other hand, many feared that a wave of tourists would ensue and ruin the very assets that attracted them. Still others felt that the government was wrongly intervening to block the sorely needed opportunities the area's growing popularity was bringing to it. In response, they organized citizen action groups and fought a nine-year battle against the legislation.

The final version of *The Sleeping Bear Sand Dunes Act* was passed by Congress in 1970, placing the area under the control of the National Park Service. It gave the Secretary of the Interior the power to purchase or condemn all private land within the park. Owners of residences could negotiate lease-backs, or could retain ownership of their residences in the park, subject to local zoning. Contrary to usual National Park Service policy, hunting would continue to be permissible in the area. The project was now called *The Sleeping Bear Dunes National Lakeshore*.

At various times during the struggle to create the park, its proponents came up with wildly inflated economic projections suggesting that the area would benefit handsomely from money spent by over 3-million seasonal visitors. That strategy had worked well in certain other areas, but it didn't work in Leelanau County. Many of the most vocal and powerful detractors were affluent seasonal residents, who came here for peace and privacy, not profit.

As the battle over the park dragged on, attitudes about development and the environment began to change throughout the country. By the end on the 1960's a new radical environmentalism had developed. Between the times the act was originally passed and a workable management plan appeared, more than ten years of hard wrangling had ensued. But the fighting was not over yet.

The original act called for the preservation of the aspects that made the region so special. That meant different things to different people. Ordinary people familiar with the area envisioned the preservation of its special charm and ambiance. To environmentalists, it meant "wilderness"; the term employed in its most academic sense, envisioning a wild and uninhabited area left in its natural condition, with no evidence of a human presence, or of man's ever having been present.

An unexpected coalition developed, pairing environmentalists with the affluent and influential property owners. The latter reasoned that the newly passed *Wilderness Act* would require that the Lakeshore be managed in a way that would discourage the hoards of tourists they feared. Although the initial reports of early park managers reflected their opinion that the Lakeshore didn't have any areas of the kind envisioned in the Wilderness Act, the coalition succeeded in having large chunks of the new park's territory designated as either proposed wilderness or potential wilderness.

In the end, that became the primary thrust of the Park Service's early management plans. Construction completed more recently than 1964 was expeditiously condemned and removed, as were other uses not considered in harmony with the character of the land. Anything else that was not considered historically important was permitted to molder until safety concerns justified its final demolition and removal.

The Manitou Passage began its slow return to an earlier time.

# The Sleeping Bear Dunes National Lakeshore

Since its inception over four decades ago, the new National Park in Leelanau County has attracted visitors in increasing numbers every year. First-time visitors are usually moved to rave about its attributes and return to share them with relatives and friends. Each year, new websites pop up, authored by visitors who feel moved to share this best kept secret with others.

Over a million visitors happily contribute tens of millions of dollars to local economies each year, yet there are few places in the park where one might encounter a crowd and "a crowd" by Sleeping Bear standards usually involves only a hundred people or so. There is no waiting in line for anything. The park is large enough that most places seem deserted, and can be appreciated as if provided especially for

one's own private enjoyment. There is hardly a direction the eyes can wander where they'll not be rewarded with a picture-postcard vista.

This is an outdoors place that has something of interest to offer to everyone. Strangers to the area enjoy auto touring, backpacking, bird watching, boating, camping, cross country skiing, fishing, hiking, hunting, interpretive programs, kayaking, nature walks, scuba diving, snorkeling, snowshoeing, stargazing, swimming, wilderness areas, and wildlife viewing. Those having family roots here enjoy revisiting old home places, often with younger family members, and rediscovering memories.

Most of the Park's day use activities cost nothing. There is no general entrance fee and, except for specific activities such as camping, the scenic dune drive and island visits, permits are not needed. Families can enjoy much of what the park has to offer at little expense beyond the price of a tank of gas, and most of these activities are equally enjoyable by both adults and children of all ages.

In the late 1950's and early 1960's, before the coming of the park, signs began to pop up everywhere in the area – "No Trespassing" – "Private Beach" – "Private Road." These represented attempts by those affluent enough to do so to purchase their little piece of this paradise. The signs, and those who owned them, are now are all gone. In making such a place, it seems unlikely indeed that the Great Spirit would have had in mind only a privileged few.

The original purpose of the early park proposals was to preserve the scenic beauty and peaceful character of the area for everyone to enjoy equally. In spite of – or perhaps partly because of – all the contention and squabbling that has accompanied its de-

*50    The Manitou Passage Story*

velopment, this goal has been largely achieved. The Manitou Passage is now mostly public property. It belongs to each one of us, and to all of us.

It seems appropriate that its history should end here.

# Bibliography

Williams, Alanen and Tishler. 1966. <u>Coming Through With Rye, An Historic Agricultural Landscape Study of South Manitou Island at Sleeping Bear Dunes National Lakeshore, Michigan</u>. Omaha, Nebraska: Midwest Field Area, National Park Service.

Anderson, Charles M. 1979. <u>Isle Of View, A History of South Manitou Island</u>. Frankfort, Michigan: JB Publications.

Crowner, Gerald E. 1982. <u>The South Manitou Story</u>. Mio, Michigan: The Print Shop.

Karamanski, Theodore J. 2000. <u>A Nationalized Lakeshore: The Creation and Administration of Sleeping Bear Dunes National Lakeshore</u>. Online ~ http://www.cr.nps.gov/history/online_books/slbe/index.htm : Department of the Interior, National Park Service

McEnaney, Tishler and Alanen. 1995. <u>Farming At the Water's Edge, An Assessment of Agricultural and Cultural Landscape Resources in the Proposed Port Oneida Rural Historic District at Sleeping Bear Dunes National Lakeshore, Michigan</u>. Omaha, Nebraska: Midwest Field Area, National Park Service.

Rader, Robert D. 1977. <u>Beautiful Glen Arbor Township; Facts, Fantasy & Fotos</u>. Glen Arbor, Michigan: Glen Arbor History Group.

Ratigan, William. 1960. <u>Great Lakes Shipwrecks & Survivals</u>. Grand Rapids, Michigan: Wm B Eerdmans Publishing Company.

Rogers, Joseph A. 1989. <u>Visitor's Guide to South Manitou Island</u>. Mason, Michigan: Maritime Press.

Ruchhoft, R H. 1991. <u>Exploring North Manitou, South Manitou, High and Garden Islands of the Lake Michigan Archipelago</u>. Cincinnati: The Pucelle Press.

Sodders, Betty. 1977. <u>Michigan on Fire</u>. San Diego: Thunder Bay Press.

Vent, Myron H. 1999. <u>South Manitou Island, From Pioneer Community to National Park</u>. Eastern National.

Vent, Wm E and Myron H. 1990. <u>Pioneer Tales and Other Stories of South Manitou Island.</u> Aurora, Illinois: J W Reproductions Inc.

# INDEX

Algonquin. *See* Paleo-Indians
American Revolution, 11
Black Sunday, 25, 27
Burton, William
   as lightkeeper, 29
   wood merchant, 21
Burton's Wharf, 22
calm, 18
canals, 13
Chicago, 13
Chippewa. *See* Paleo-Indians
chop and slash, 25
Clinton, Dewitt, 13
Clinton's Folly, 13
Crescent Bay, 22
   as refuge, 30
Ericsson, John, 19
Erie Canal, 13
European immigration, 36
farming, 37
Firestorms, 27
Forest and brush fires. *See* Black Sunday
French and Indian War, 9
*Frontenac*, 17
Fur Trade, 7
   British, 9
German immigrants, 35
glaciers, 1
Glen Haven, 25
government workers, 30

Great Lakes
   formation, 1
   shipping, 14
*Great Manitou*, 5
Great Spirit. *See* Manitou
Hamilton, Alexander, 17
Hart, Phillip A, 44
Hurons. *See* Woodland Indians
Indians. *See* Native Americans
Iroquois, 8
Iroquois League, 8
Jesuit priests, 8
Keeper (lighthouse), 30
Kelderhouse, Thomas, 24
Lake Michigan
   early navigation, 7
   formation of, 1
   maritime era, 29
Lands Reserved for the Indians. *See* Fur Trade
Leelanau County, 44
Leland, 22
Life Saving Station, 32
Lighthouse Service, 30
lighthouses, 29
   on North Manitou, 32
*Little Manitou*, 5
locomotives, 26
Manitou, 5
*Manitou* (lightship), 32
Manitou Passage, 2, 29
   first lighthouses, 29

trade route, 14
maritime disasters, 31
McCarthy, Charles, 24
*Michelite Bean*, 39
Michigan
  "no man's land", 8
  pre-settlement, 4
Michigan State University
  on South Manitou Island, 38
*Mishimigobing*
  See Leland, 22
National Park Service, 45
Native Americans, 3
Nipissing. *See* Paleo-Indians
North Manitou Island, 15
  first ghost town, 24
  wooding stations, 23
Northern Transportation Company, 25
*Northwest Territory*, 11
Ojibwa. *See* Woodland Indians
Ottawa. *See* Woodland Indians
packets, 14
Paleo-Indians, 3
Pickard, Nicholas, 23
Port Oneida, 24
  farming era, 39
Potawatomi. *See* Woodland Indians
pre-historic peoples, 3
propellers, 19
Pyramid Point, 24

railroads, 26
Recruiters, immigration, 36
Rosen Rye, 39
*S. S. Oneida*, 24
sawdust, 26
screw propeller, 19
settlements, 29
settlers, 35
Settlers
  European, 7
  French, 7
Seven Years War, 9, 35
shipwrecks, 25, 30, 31
shoals, 15, 30
Sleeping Bear Bay, 30
Sleeping Bear Dunes, 44
Sleeping Bear Dunes National Lakeshore, 33, 45
  a National Park, 49
  and environmentalism, 46
  and histori preservation, 46
  and wilderness, 46
  struggle to develop, 45
*Sleeping Bear Sand Dunes Act*, 45
Sleeping Bearville. *See* Glen Haven
South Manitou Island
  as refuge, 14
  as wooding station, 21
steamboat, 21
steamers, 19
steamships, 18, 25

stovewood, 21
Surfmen, 33
The Day Michigan Burned. *See* Black Sunday
*Thirty Years War*, 35
tourism, 41
   development of, 44
United States Coast Guard, 32
*United States Life Saving Service*, 31
*Vandalia*, 18
*Walk-In-The-Water*, 17
War of 1812, 11
wilderness. *See* Sleeping Bear Dunes National Lakeshore
   pre-settlement, 1
*Wilderness Act*, 46
wood merchants, 37
wooding, 21, 25
wooding stations, 21
Woodland Indians, 4
World War II, 41

# About the Author

Gene Warner began life on South Manitou Island,[1] as the first son of Coast Guardsman Lonzo Warner and former island teacher Myrtle Kelderhouse; grandson of August and Rosie Warner of South Manitou, and William and Charlotte Kelderhouse, of Port Oneida. His ancestry therefore traces back to immigrant island settlers George Conrad Hutzler and George Haas, and to the pioneering Thomas Kelderhouse, founder of Port Oneida.

His life-long love affair with what he embraced, even at that young age, as Michigan's very own paradise, began as a boy of the 1940's and 50's, filling summer days with wonder and adventure on the island and in the Port Oneida area.

The Warners reside in Grand Haven, Michigan.

---

[1] Weather permitting, the Island's expectant mothers were taken to the mainland when the blessed event seemed imminent. Actual place of birth ~ Munson Hospital, Traverse City, Michigan, September 23, 1940.

Works by Gene Warner ...

### *The Manitou Passage Story*
An Indefinitive History of the Settlement of Northeast Lake Michigan.

### *Solutions for Secretaries of Small NPO's*
A guide for nonprofit corporate secretaries and administrative assistants. Learn how to build a first class image on a third rate budget.

### *Mind Over Monster*
A book for boys – about thinking rationally and constructively to provide a highly successful, abundantly happy and richly rewarding life.

### *Manitou Passage People*
A fictional remembrance of life in the Manitou Passage, loosely based upon some historical fact, but as colored by traditional hearsay and exaggerations.

### *South Island*
Fiction – a murder mystery that might cast a chill on your youth group's camping plans.

*BoysMind Books*
PO Box 604
Grand Haven, MI 49417-0604 USA
www.boysmindbooks.com

www.ingramcontent.com/pod-product-compliance
Lightning Source LLC
Chambersburg PA
CBHW071841290426
44109CB00017B/1898